What people are saying about
WRITTEN EYE: VISUALS/VERSE

"Somewhere between what we see and what that vision asks of us, is poetry. In art's reciprocal space A. Robert Lee's *Written Eye: Visuals/ Verse* lingers, bringing to readers "entrance words" to engage their own "witness eye." This catalogue of seeing, this caressing litany of artistic encounters across continents takes us from the surfaces of photographs, film, sculpture, architecture, and painting to their interior reverberations—and ours. Lee's poetry brings to this "feast of angle" a wealth of knowledge, an eye for striking detail, and a poet's questions. From Georgia O'Keeffe to Ai Weiwei, the Parthenon to Prague, take this tour: *This is imagination alive, exhaling.*"

—Kimberly Blaeser, Wisconsin Poet Laureate,
author of *Apprenticed to Justice*

"A. Robert Lee's enquiring eye roams over paintings, photographs, sculptures, movies, buildings and cityscapes. Whether in occident or orient, whether surveying a railway station or the Acropolis, whatever he sees he describes, quizzes, probes, challenges, contextualizes—and relishes. Sometimes he notices the quirky, the absurd, the improbable, the outrageous, the stunning. Occasionally, he gapes, astonished. From time to time his heart is warmed by the familiar, the undramatic, the quotidian. In each and every text, he picks the locks of vision. Through multiple modes of seeing, these vignettes and meditations reveals a rich, varied world, brimming with energy and delight."

—Richard Berengarten
author of *Under Balkan Light,* Cambridge, UK.

"A. Robert Lee in his new collection of poetry, *Written Eye,* shows what an eclectic mind can do when viewing painting, photography, film, sculpture and architecture. Paintings, by such opposed sensibilities as Turner and Rothko are seized upon and given Lee's genial but loaded

commentary. He illuminates just what stands behind the artist and the work in personal anecdotes—with considerable artlessness and often funny too! Unpretentious in style: an authentic voice that we hear vividly on each page."

"What a feast for the senses! A. Robert Lee's verse courageously explores the pinnacles of artistic achievement; the fragments of a whole that kaleidoscope and then coalesce in the mind's eye. I felt as though I had traveled the globe, a witness to some of the finest spectacles humanity has offered."

"A. Robert Lee's *Written Eye* is a wonderful exercise in the ancient art of ekphrasis: the literary re-enactment of a work of art. Lee takes us on a visual journey spanning all the arts—painting, photography, film, sculpture and architecture, pondering and exploring the ways and skills of seeing. His rich language and eye of curiosity makes for his own art history book. These texts are beautiful and full of interest in their own right."

Written Eye: Visuals/Verse

Written Eye: Visuals/Verse

A Poetry Collection by A. Robert Lee

NEW YORK

www.2leafpress.org

P.O. Box 4378
Grand Central Station
New York, New York 10163-4378
editor@2leafpress.org
www.2leafpress.org

2LEAF PRESS
is an imprint of the
Intercultural Alliance of Artists & Scholars, Inc. (IAAS),
a NY-based nonprofit 501(c)(3) organization that promotes
multicultural literature and literacy.
www.theiaas.org

Cover art, book design and layout: Gabrielle David

Library of Congress Control Number: 2016951240
ISBN-13: 978-1-940939-59-9 (Paperback)
ISBN-13: 978-1-940939-60-5 (eBook)

10 9 8 7 6 5 4 3 2 1

Published in the United States of America

First Edition | First Printing

2LEAF PRESS trade distribution is handled by University of Chicago Press / Chicago Distribution Center (www.press.uchicago.edu), 773.702.7000. Titles are also available for corporate, premium, and special sales. Please direct inquiries to the UCP Sales Department, 773.702.7248.

For Andy Sotiriou (and camera)

Contents

SCULPTURE :: 101

ARCHITECTURE :: 123

Introduction

For the eye altering, alters all.

—William Blake

Realism is not tenable. You have to write a poem about what you are describing.

—Robert Stone

VISUALS. VERSE. Together they refract encounters that for one reason or another and over the years have caught and then held my eye. I hope readers of *Written Eye* will hie to the originals that give rise to these poems, a variety of pleasures in their own right. Almost all are to be found in image on the web. In some cases I have concentrated on the single work or edifice. In others I have tried for the broad span, the fuller reach of a group of works, or a scenario in its multiple aspects, or a city. In whichever case the aim has been the same: to see and voice.

By way of opening are touchstones from three continents. Three landmarks of seeing and the seen. Nazca. Buddha. Bayeux.

The compositions that follow, each in sequences of a dozen, seek to work as ekphrasis.

Paintings as pigment and signature. Photo-shots as aperture and grammar. Film as image and style. Sculpture as mass and vernacular. Architecture as construct and form.

A span, I hope, of international sight and saying.

None of these choices is to imply some simply best-of, a canon. Rather, they have each entered my own reckoning by their singularity. High or popular. Not to say pitched somewhere between. And always by the invitation to have eye and word collaborate. ❏

Prologue

Art does not reproduce, rather it makes visible.

—Paul Klee

Eyes Down:
"Las Líneas de Nazca"

Desert Peru seen from Economy Class.
What gods or formations are these below?
Do here be dragons you kind of ask.
And even as you select pasta or chicken.
Or take advantage of the wine list.

A feast of tribal imagination.
Cartography markings.
Landing runways. Time trails.
Trapezium, grid.
Sun, star and cross geo-glyph.

Deities? Sky messengers?
Or, *milagrito,* the extra-terrestrial.
Imagined galaxy visitors.
Welcomes, homage, awaiting worship.
Perhaps, you fantasize, to yourself looking downward.

You look closer.
Hummingbird and Spider.
Pelican and Monkey.
Ocean orca, rock lizard.
Historiae animalium.

Calendars? Canals?
Handprints. Suction feet.
Coil, spine, wing, silhouette.
Scraped pebble red to reveal white.
Earth as palette.

You in window seat.
Now the avian visitor.
Guest or god privilege.
Eyeing art's enigma.
Eyeing art's earthwork.

Steady Eye:
"The Great Buddha of Nara"

i.
Some of Buddhism you think you see.
Mantra, wheel, lotus, karma.
The repose, harmony, even the ears.
You learn Siddhartha Gautama.
You read Herman Hesse.
You look to awake Buddhas.
You regard Buddhas at rest or seated.
You think world Buddhas, cosmos.
You travel in mind through heaven and earth.
But your eye remains that of visitor.

ii.
How, best, to see what's there to see?
There are Buddhas you have still to learn.
Silk Road cave Buddha.
Tang Dynasty Leshan river Buddha.
Hong Kong Lantau Island Buddha.
Phuket white marble Buddha.
Taichung smiling Golden Buddha.
Bihar Bodhgaya meditation Buddha.
Korea Mount Sorak Buddha.
Bamiyan Taliban-lost Buddha.

iii.
So you keep looking.
Twice-over in Japan.
First the Kamakura Buddha.
Robe-folded, seated.
Kōtoku-in Temple.

Mountain backdrop.
Daibutsu. Giant Buddha.
Amida. Celestial.
The entrance words.
Gateway to the Eternal.

iv.
Then you look south.
Kansai by *shinkansen*.
Nara. Ancient capital.
Icon Japan.
Tōdai-ji. East Temple.
The Great Buddha.
Nara Daibutsu.
Tranquility's face.
Spread hand of peace.
The gaze afar.

v.
You stay, look, try again to see.
Acolyte, no, but eye engaged.
Eighth century time.
Presence yet distance.
Copper, bronze.
Pillars of harmony.
Force, sun, colossus.
Birushani.
A power of sight and guidance.
The invitation to yet more seeing.

Eye of the Needle:
"The Bayeux Tapestry"

Tapisserie de Bayeux.
The stitch and weave of history.
Chronology sumptuously medieval.
Norman helmet. Saxon axe.
French Normandy. English Wessex.
William. Harold. Hastings.
Ship. Horse. Armor. Shield. Mace.
Battlefield cut and thrash.

Equivocation shadows truth to fact.
Heirships to crown.
Harold Godwinson's arrow death.
William's legitimate kingship.
Bishop Odo as player.
English army flight.
Norman pillage.
Victor history?

But this is mural, fifty strips.
Queen Matilda and ladies at needle.
Invasion as embroidery, hem and linen.
Human face and body figure-drawn.
Animal and hunt borders.
Halley's Comet burst.
Latin *tituli,* wool-woven, blue-black.
Terracotta, olive, reds, russets.

Museum Bayeux.
Design, needle, craft.
You visit, look, admire.

Truth to history? Maybe.
Summoned event yet invention.
Time in imagined pattern.
Art's roll. Art's vision.
And your own witness eye.

Painting

There can be no doubt that there is something peculiar in the condition of the English retina.

Said Taine, viewing a first exhibition of Pre-Raphaelite art.

—David Markson
This is Not a Novel (2001)

Right There:
Vermeer's "View of Delft"

Gezicht op Delft
Schie river. Rotterdam Gate.
Herring boat repair.
Barge, mast, prow.
Gates and barbican.
Quayside yellow. Roof tile red.
Fallen rain.

Gezicht op Delft.
Dutch Republic confidence.
The settled townscape.
The solid burgher encounters.
Things in their place.
Things, well, a picture.
Exactness.

Gezicht op Delft.
Dutch golden age for sure.
But idyll hinting of disturbance.
Repose yet looming cloud.
River-calm yet hint of eddies.
Citizen ease yet in for a shock.
Calm and un-calm in tension.

Gezicht op Delft
The experts pronounce.
Photo-real but not quite.
Civic-real but not quite.
Vista adjusted.

Perspective altered.
The artist's eye craft.

Gezicht op Delft.
The gaze lingers, ponders.
Each muted ochre, umber.
Gradations of Colour.
The feast of angle.
The visual poetry.
Beauteous, elided, contrary.

Floating: Hiroshige

*it was one of his favorite Hiroshiges...graceful calligraphy,
a sea that was pale blue except for the edges...pine-
dotted mountains of grey and blue.*

—Hisaye Yamamoto, "Seventeen Syllables"

Step into Edo Japan.
Be seated under *sakura*.
Stroll river bank.
Watch the carp-kite.

Hanging willow branch.
Resting crane.
Walkway bridge.
Fuji-san vista.

Season changes.
Parasol and umbrella.
Walkers under sun, under snow.
The exquisite impression.

Temple, pagoda, bell.
Iris, ripple, pine.
Plum tree, whirlpool, horseback.
Eyed variety, the draftsman's precision.

Ukiyo-e: each a landscape, a seascape, afloat.
Woodblock: each a line, grace.
Tableau: each a face, figure, tint, script.
Hiroshige: each a master image, skill.

Curvature: Cézanne's "Bends"

i.
River Bend (1865)
Coin de rivière
Shadow-dark sighting.
Thick-oil coloration.
Deep-bold stroke.
River run and turn.
Tree presence, rock force.
Sky movement. Greenery.
Painted, saturated, My God, touch the paint.
Even the bank-side figure.

ii.
The Bend Through the Forest (1873-5)
La Route tournante en sous-bois
Insistent leaf green.
Insistent sky blue.
Rightward wheel track path.
Leftward lean of tree and branch.
Homestead turn of corner cottage.
A touch of breeze?
Early Spring flower?
Pastoral just about to leave the real.

iii.
A Bend of the Road (1900)
Un virage de la route
Beyond post-impressionism, swab, swirl.
Almost cubism, wash and block.

Roadway light patina.
Tree bodies a family blur.
Bank, forest, hill, sky a colour menu.
Locale yes but far more.
Brushstrokes gestural, approximate.
The road towards abstraction.

Cut-Out: Matissse

*La main n'est que le prolongement de la sensibilité
et de l'intelligence.*
*The hand is only an extension of sensitivity and
intelligence.*

—Matisse, Notebook

Dancing beauty.
Gymnastic prism.
Scissored kaleidoscope.

Matisse speaking.
"Cutting directly into colour."
"Abstraction rooted in reality."

Fern, tendril, star.
Gouache patterns.
Glued clusters.

Technique doesn't say enough.
These are walls of life.
Figurings of breath.

Kinetic pallets.
Swirl and gust of blue or red or green.
Plays of light and pattern.

You look at *Jazz* and *Verve*.
You read the journals.
Illustration and text junctured into art.

But the eye fixes always upon the image.
The ballet of blue nude dancers.
Icarus un-waxed and falling.

Each cut-out a vision, transcendent.
Oceana fish, coral, bird flights.
Vence studio forms of plant and leaf.

There's Tahiti, Morocco, Creole Africa.
The Parakeet and Mermaid.
And that gyred, unfolding snail.

His *Chapelle du Rosaire de Vence* goes bolder,
An unbeliever's Jesus, Mary, Saint.
The luminosity of glass cut-out.

Large *Decoration with Masks* offers a gathering.
Late age perfection. Illness's rebuke.
Himself the cut-out of Art's summons.

In-gallery, or even catalogue, the colours hold.
A magic of paper, embossment, pigment.
This is imagination alive, exhaling.

How not to re-see those hands at work?
Shape, composition, hue, light.
The scissoring of vision.

Bridging: J.M.W. Turner's "Rain, Steam, and Speed– The Great Western Railway"

Skyline, cloud, wave, storm.
Land and sea, the canvas-scapes hold you.
Luminosity, the see-through blur, impasto.
Turner fare and vision.

The slave thrown overboard. Trafalgar's *Temeraire*.
Sunrise sea monsters all opportune gullet.
Canalled Chichester and Venice.
The vortex of *Snow Storm*. The bible of *The Deluge*.

Each its spectrum, each its sublime prism.
Genesis or no, *Light and Colour* speaks.
The painter's own language.
Abstract precision.

Rain, Steam and Speed.
Almost odd to see the iron train.
Technology's speed through the downpour.
And Brunel's Maidenhead bridge.

Funnel, carriage, a screeching track.
Soot, sound, passenger excitement.
The river, the bank, the horizon.
Pastoral, a boat to remind of ebb.

Scale, the composition's balance.
Fierce engine thrust, sky-swirl.
Arched viaduct, land's edge.
Turner's daring brushstroke command.

John Singer Sargent: "Robert Louis Stevenson and His Wife"

A perfect gauntness, dark, puckered.
You might say just one of myriad Sargent portraits.

I mean you travel the commissioned faces and figures.
Madame This, The Honorable That.
John D. Rockefeller, Marquess de Curzon.
Astors and Vanderbilts, Cabot Lodge and Teddy Roosevelt.
Ellen Terry, the Sitwells.
Gilded Age bounty. Edwardian deluxe.
It's brushstroke realism, keen exactness.
Not least his king-bearded self portraits.

There are the English landscapes.
You can eye the Mediterranean water colours.
Plein air scene, gondolier, and olive grove.
Simplon Pass, Venice street, Tyrol stream.
Corfu terrace, Jardin de Luxembourg.

Bodies, too, male, muscled, mural sketches.
Egyptian girl nude.

You can discern impressionism's just-about touch.
Claude Monet Painting by the Edge of the Woods.
Millet's Garden. Garden Fantasy. Alpine Pool.
Yet a man of his time, the 1880s and after, passé by the 1920s.
Europe's American, along with Whistler and James.

Then you turn again to *Stevenson and His Wife.*
So much more than just one of the myriad plenty.
The portrait almost haunts itself.
"Damn queer" said Stevenson.
Maybe, but maybe just right.
The consumed look, the fidget, the half-turn.
Where is he going? The door and stairway of imagination?
And Fanny, Klimt shawl-covered, waiting, fed up?

This isn't formal pose but writer at thought.
A room the colour of displacement, otherness.
Where Jekyll and Hyde might have been conjured.

Stevenson's looking at being seen.
Sargent's rare enduring figuration.

Vienna Modern: "Egon Schiele (Leopold Collection)"

For Cathy Waegner

i.
Schiele portraying Schiele
Scrawny brilliance.
Jags of physiology.
Expressionist verve.
Torque.

Selbstbildnis mit hochgezogener nackter Schulter
Self-Portrait with Raised Bare Shoulder
The brushwork bold, daubed, thick.
Just right for that defensive left shoulder.
Add in the swirl of face, the forehead scar.
The eyes stare large, oval.
The open mouth promises sound, a cry.
Hair, ear, neck, throat give diagonals.
If flinch, retreat, you sense also could-be attack.
Art, the artist, in combat with life.

Selbstbildnis mit gesentktem kopf
Self-Portrait with Lowered Head
What face to see?
Rebuke, misery?
The head tilts and leans.
The forehead almost landslides the eyes.
The cheeks turn in on themselves.
The tash looks military-prim.
The chin settles accusingly.
The fingers sprawl.

Skeletal, knuckle-red.
The clothing almost a nightshirt.
The artist defying his own pose.

Männlicher Unterleibstorso
Male Lower Body Torso
Legs stationed like satyr stilts.
Blue, mauve, the hint of hirsute.
Spine sprung back as if to hold balance.
Rump an uneven promontory.
Knee-joints each an armor brace.
Groin of genital red, pubic black.
Four dangling finger ends.
Elongated, downward.
Parts a whole yet un-whole.
Commanding a-symmetry.

Selbstbildnis mit Hemd
Self-Portrait with Shirt
Hands that point and pinion.
Leg stalks of inner down.
Shock of flamed hair.
Eyes all red stare and focus.
But the garment a void.
Un-tucked, odd-sleeved.
The outside drape over the familiar within.

Selbstbildnis in schwarzem Gewand
Self-Portrait in Black Garment
Black verticals of brushstroke.
Funereal. Poe. Baudelaire.
Socketed eyes.
Cheekbone gauntness.
Kerchief and frock coat.

Knuckled flesh of fingers.
Upright pose.
Chill formality.
The ghost of himself.

Selbstsdarstellung, grimmassierend
Self-Portrait, Grimacing
Maybe but the mouth, the square tooth, the raised brows
have you thinking worse.
Ogre, madman, werewolf.
Maybe but the breastbone, the scrunched face,
have you thinking otherwise.
The face of distemper, wildness, threat.
Maybe, but the open shirt, the tawny flesh
have you thinking more.
The body's composed gnarl.

Halbakt (Selbstdarstellung)
Semi-Nude (Self-Portrait)
Diagonal, almost a death.
Catatonic eyes.
Given over visage.
Body sloped into dissolve.
As though the paint,
the tints of flesh and costume,
were un-congealing
into resignation, despair.

Selbstdarstellung mit gestreiften Ärmelschonern
Self-Portrait with Striped Oversleeves
Jester, unstringed puppet.
The blaze of orange hair.
The cocked head.
The wide-eyed stare.

The akimbo arms.
Zebra sleeves.
Counter uniform.
Each a mis-signal.
Each an anti-rotation.
The very tilt of the artist.
The harlequin in sight of himself.

ii.
Egon Schiele and Wally Neuzil
Inter-faces.
Inter-bodies.
One. Two. One again.

Selbstbildnis mit Lampionfrüchten
Self-portrait with Chinese Lantern Plant
Dilated eye stare. Listen ready ear.
Rightward neck tilt. Down sloped shoulder.
Thick hair crop itself cropped by frame.
Kinetic energy of face, gaze, vision.
Corporeal thickness of line and pigment.
Ornamental hanging bladder fruit, stalk and leaf.
The artist's readiness in and for his art.

Bildnis Wally Neuzil
Portrait of Wally Neuzil.
Rounded blue of retina. Exposed height of cheek.
Leftward incline of head.
Gown so elegantly white laced of collar.
Watched, composed, costumed.
The ochre hair, the play of rouge.
Again the ornament of plant stem.
The lover model in and for her reflection.

Liebespaar
Lovers
Embodied. Each other's.
Rapt. Entwined.
Faces displaced.
Shared grasp of arm.
Lips pursed.
Egon's brown waistcoat. Wally's red blouse.
Mere temporary imprisoning
of legs, breast, pubis.
Intimacies.
Less contrast than juncture.
Compare *Liebesakt/Lovemaking.*
Embrace in orange, brown, green.
The very sexuality, even fatigue, of love.

iii.
Schiele women
Sexual?
Well, yes.
Squats, spread legs, genitals.
But you wouldn't say arch.
No knowing wink or come-on pout.
Figured, painted, as if insouciance.
Nude, even only part-exposed, the female form trouvé.
For Schiele, doubtless, a fixation.
But, for viewers all, take it as you will.
Body art, the utter unsettling art of body.

Rothaariges Mädchen in schwarzem Kleid mit gespreizten Beinen.
Red-Haired Girl in Black Dress with Spread Legs.
I suppose there's a power of invitation.
Knees raised, skirt lifted.
On her back, eyes elsewhere.
The black of dress.

The red-orange of hair, lip, garter, vagina.
The hint of garment green.
But she is as much for herself as you.

Mädchen mit übereinandergeschlagenen Beinen
Girl with Crossed Legs
Seated, staring back, at ease.
Feline visage, rouge lips.
Red-brown skirt askew.
Limbs black stocking'd, red garter'd.
White bloomers half open.
Hands folded on hip.
The sitter in her oval chair.
Monitoring her own coloration.

Schwarzhaariges Mädchen mit hochgeschlagenem Rock
Black-Haired Girl with Lifted Skirt
Closed eyes.
You might again think she herself were elsewhere.
But not her in body.
Flagrant vagina, matching mouth.
Wild bonnet of hair.
Kneeled and back-leaning pose.
Billow of skirt.
Hint of under-slip.
Upper and Lower.
Light and dark.
Gouache flow of composition.
Life posture. Art posture.
Her fantasy. His fantasy.
Each outside and inside the other.

Stehendes nacktes Mädchen mit orangefarbenen Strümpfen
Standing Nude Girl with Orange Stockings
Almost warrior stance.
Upright. Symmetried.

Pendant arms. Legs braced.
Triangle neck. Concentrated stare.
Collar bone line.
Breast bone ripple.
Skin tone white.
Then that orange body tapestry.
Lips, nipples, rumpled stockings.
Geometric umbilicus and pubis.
Figure drawing?
Utterly, absolutely.
A feat.

Kniende auf rotem Polster
Girl Kneeling on Red Cushion
The neck bends forward.
The arm slopes down.
The ribs show in their turn.
The knees touch bed.
Red lips reach to between-legs red cushion.
Angle and inclination.
Line and twist of body.
Line and motion of drawing.
We watch and tilt with her.
Lightness of being if close then distant.

Kniende in orange-rotem Kleid
Kneeling Female in Orange-Red Dress
His own knelt sister as Carmen?
Wraps of flame.
Swirl. Fold.
Funnels of dress, hair.
Forehead hand.
Blue-alert eye.
Splayed boots.
Live figurine.
Orange-red beauteous.

iv.
Schiele landscapes
Haus mit Schindeldach
House with Shingle Roof
So exactly shingle-squared.
Yet fading into mausoleum.
So exactly shingle-squared.
Yet patterning into decay.
You could think the shingles book rows.
Or mosaic about to un-tile.
The serial lines suggest warp, sag.
Windows out of balance.
Gapped and spindly fence.
Crumbling pillars.
The laundry almost token.
Melancholic brown, autumn aged.
A house of life near death.

Hauswand am Fluss
House Wall by River
Façade. Veranda.
Hermetic. Weighted.
Bolted windows.
The rows might be prisoner cells.
The heaviness reflects in the water.
No call to nostalgia, fond lyric.
Residence as though in absentia.
Only a brief clothesline of life.

Versinkende Sonne
Setting Sun
Move down the canvas.
Summer's end. Day's end.
Withdrawing heat and colour.
Bare islands, stark trees.

Gloomed terrain, black earth.
You have good reason to think transition.
The chill of exit.
The palette's shades compel.
Distant light to near dark.
Corridors of darkening hue.
Life's fade and fall.

v.

Schiele art

Der Lyriker
The Poet
Sideways on.
Oblique, a brilliant contortion.
Art, that is, and Schiele.
That self-face right to left.
That dark cloak.
Those clasped and thumbless hands.
The penile red.
The thick oil, the figuring strokes.
You think of his plethora.
Galleries of body and landscape.
You think of *Die Familie.*
Love over death.
Contour, parent-child tenderness.
You think of *Tote Mutter1*
Pallid death face.
Womb child life.
You think of *Mutter under Tochter*
Red-clad mother
Loving daughter embrace.
You think of *Liebkosung.*
Cardinal and nun religio-erotica.
Counter-kiss to Klimt
You think of his letters.

Epistles as box, cartouche.
Calligraphy almost haiku.
The painter-poet.
Absorbed.
Tensile.
Angle and line.
Darkness yet light.
Torque.

American Colours:
Georgia O'Keeffe's "Cow Skull"

Those flowers, leaf and bulb.
Sexual, tactile, swirl and fold.
Petals. Fragrance.
Almost personal to you.

Jack in the Pulpit, an opening.
Calla Lilly, virgin field.
Oak Leaves, love holds.
Petunias, blood lips.
White Rose with Larkspur, natural linen.
Pineapple Bud, early start.
Oriental Poppies, your assignations.

Floral erotica. Precise.
O'Keeffe's beckoning touch shall we say.

Those landscapes, hill and mesa.
A southwest of browns, rusts.
Rock terrace, pueblo and sunflower.
Heat shimmer, cliff shadow.

Cow Skull: Red, White and Blue.
Patriot colours but a worn-in land.
No epic prospect or canyon.
No fresh green breast.
Cattle trail, rather, horns, jaw.
Dinner plate America.
Full of graze, weather, local time.

Bone country. Precisionist.
O'Keefe's winning tease.

Migration Series:
Jacob Lawrence

In memoriam, John A. Williams

Most of my work depicts scenes from the many Harlems which exist throughout the United States.

—Jacob Lawrence

i.
What tribute.
Three score panels.
Blues trek.
Stepping north.
Train whistle.
Cotton Dixie to the cities.
Harlem, Chicago, St. Louis.

What tribute.
Three score panels.
Blues train.
Field sack to brownstone stoop.
Profile, family, life, death.
Black being.
Black truth.

ii.
What tribute.
A dazzle of craft.
Mural savvy, styling.
Pigments thick, sharp, full.
Face and figure a boldest colour-chart.
Silhouette and word a shared poem.
His art of face and figure.

What tribute.
See all, see each, unfold.
Scenario of crop and lynch.
Tableau of train and leave-taking.
Vista of tenement, factory, riot.
Sight-line of street, jailhouse, vote.
His art of line and block.

What tribute.
You could read the histories.
You could listen to Ellington.
You could alight on texts of Hughes or Ellison.
But with the *Series* you can watch.
Visible hue, precision graphic.
His art of America's Afro-journey.

Cuban Africa:
Wilfredo Lam's "Madame Lu-
mumba"

Misalignments it could be said.
The portrait's titling not Lam's own.
Fashioned the 1930s not the 1960s.
The Congo's Lumumba name a retrofit.

Alignments it could be said.
Lam's Canton and Kinshasa parentage.
His Afro-Cuba of slave, *santería*, magic.
The Jungle in homage to figure and mask.

No doubting he knew Africa's gift to Cubism.
His art, his surreal, a return payment.
Madrid and Paris, along with Havana, his training.
Picasso and Fidel, along with Césaire, his thread.

Madame Lumumba.
Her human geometry.
Angled face, stalk neck, bold shoulders.
Eyes in query, head tilted, ready.

Gouache cube-pigments.
Each its pastel, each a panel.
Circle and triangle an anatomy.
Visage and torso an algebra.

You look but so does she.
Querying, a stare of her own.
Maybe she knows there are debts owed.
And is saying you're welcome, or not.

Planes: Rothko

It's eventual Rothko that holds your scrutiny.
The un-titled, the numbered, to avoid all naming.
Picturing, no more, no less.
Essentials, the numinous.

Magic colour rectangles.
Soft vertical and horizontal inter-bleeds.
Call them (he did) Reds, Blues, Greys, Earth.
Elided, huge, risen.

It was time to get rid of images he said.
Now was right to have picture planes he said.
He wasn't an abstractionist he said.
The goal was transcendence he said.

"Silence is so accurate" ran the credo.
Be free of wordage, metaphor.
The planes in fact depth, an interior
Luminosity. Scale. Convergence.

You follow his pathways: Judaica. Latvia.
Nietzsche. The Greeks. Freud. Jung.
Myth. Modernism. Multiform. New York.
And then the canvases, his art's windows.

The paradoxes also draw you.
The Seagram murals to upset Four Seasons diners.
Jewish Catholicism in Houston, the Rothko Chapel.
Black on Black paintings.

The eye he demanded takes time.
As though a blink, then a lid long-time open.
The colours become field, tablet, seam.
Rothko's own seeing walls of marvel.

Scapegoating London:
Gilbert and George at White Cube

We said very early on that we never wanted to become the artists that mother would be ashamed of. It hasn't worked out anything like that.

—Gilbert and George

The sheer bloody cheek of it.
You love it. Or don't.
They themselves paired installations.
Formal-suited, deadpan, cannily rude.

Prepare yourself with their filmed "Singing Sculpture."
The both of them day-glowed in face and hand.
One voice all pucker-English, the other Italian but sounding Peter Lorre.
Their song, reflexively, "Underneath the Arches."

They enter their pageant like impresarios.
Hoodies, gas-masked, death's heads.
Watcher-Lectors or puppet-masters.
Bad Boy witnesses to New London.

Here's their city. Le Rouge et Le Noir.
Red and black at white Bermondsey Cube.
Sixty-plus, as it were, stained glass windows.
Panels of alley, wall, strip.

You cover the East End, EC2Y.
Then Bethnal Green to Wood Green.
You see the sights.
Bangla City to chauffeured royalty.

Each window motif'd in canisters.
Laughing gas London.
Nitrous oxide if you like.
Drug *du jour,* more likely *de la nuit.*

You eye the contrariety.
Burka'd women next to roast pork.
Shroud of Turin next to canister euphoria.
Islamic State next to Body Poppers.

You read the counter-graffiti.
Pope-rape, homo-gibes, dildo-speak.
You take in the titles-wit.
Smithers. Bi signs. Ich dien. Fruit Exchange.

So wall to wall, canister to canister, you go.
Bomb, cylinder, mini-blimp, crack.
Ticking London.
 City's art. Art's city.

I heard a passerby say it was Gilbert and Sullivan.
Nobody was mentioning Joseph Priestley.
The dub is "human sculptors."
The invite reads "Welcome to London."

Gilbert and George.
Motto "Beware of Artists."
Their two for one.
Red and Black.

Jihadi London. Building site London.
Terror and bigotry London.
Hints of Hogarth London.
Dada visual wit London.

Photograph

When I say I'd like to photograph someone, what it really means is I'd like to know them.

—Annie Leibovitz

Henri Cartier-Bresson: "Juvisy, France"

Technique is important only insofar as you must master it to communicate what you see.

—Cartier-Bresson

The decisive moment? For sure.
Grass bank slope.
Moored skip.
Water shadow.
River line.

Day out.
Plates and cutlery.
Spread cloth.
Serviettes, a newspaper.
Hamper, eats.

Have a picnic in the sun.
Have one plate wait another.
Have a bite, pause, settle.
Use your hands.
Pour a glass of *vin rouge*.

Two hats, two hairdos.
White tops, shirt and blouse.
Four solid worker backs.
Seated legs.
Used plate, more to come.

No static riverside.
Yes, a moment, a verge.
Yes, a perpendicular instant.
But your eye busies you downward.
The image's companion diner.

Some Kiss: Eisenstaedt's "V-J Day in Times Square"

Think about the repertoire.
The marbled clasp of Rodin's *Francesca da Rimini*.
The medieval embrace of Hayez's *The Kiss*.
The gilded intimacy of Art Nouveau's Klimt.
Add in Kitagawa's pillow, Brancusi's *Le Baiser*, Magritte's hoods.

Then Eisenstaedt.
You note each paradox.
The camera of a Jewish Polish-German.
The American once photographer of Goebbels.
The Victory over Japan in landmark Manhattan.

You contemplate photojournalist mastery.
LIFE magazine and a thousand covers.
Marilyn to JFK, Loren to Churchill.
The images inside *The Eye of Alfred Eisenstadt*.
There's "now" in his Clinton portraits.

But, always, his sailor and nurse.
Time Square street frame.
Two bodies, one there-and-then encounter.
The moment's iconic euphoria.
The spontaneous kiss of life over war, death.

Home from the sea.
Out from the ward.
Uniforms breaking rank.
Navy blue and hospital white.
Live harlequinry.

The embrace of chance.
He, she, the lens.
All held.
Swerve, seize, enrapt.
Taking history's shot.

Karsh's Auden

Portrait gallery. The term hardly suffices.
A serial of faces, sitters, notables.

Karsh of Ottawa.
Itself *une expression fixe.*
Like Arden of Faversham.
Or Ludwig of Bavaria.
Hard to remember his Armenia.
Or forename Yousuf.
Even his Order of Canada.

That gallery.
Life magazine Churchill. Young Elizabeth.
Coiffured Benazir. Ready to rumble Ali.
Pius XII under red cowl. Coquette Bardot.
Hepburn impeccable. Hemingway in roll-neck.

Studio, light, magic.
Lens and sitter a contract.
His lens a probe, a seeking.

So you pick a favourite.
Mine's 1972 Auden.
Puckish, the overgrown schoolboy.
Yet visage as craggy as mountainside.
Head and brow weighing down shoulders.
Caught mid-glance as it were.
Casual buttoned jacketed, hands in pocket.
Body thinner but hair thick.
Best verse behind him?
The hint of a life played out?
An epilogue.

Poet and portraitist.
Whose eye to watch?

Ansel Adams:
"Canyon de Chelly
National Monument"

Wherever one goes in the Southwest one encounters
magic, strength, and beauty.

—Ansel Adams

To be sure, Adams's Yosemite, the West.
But also his Southwest, 1940s and Arizona.

A portfolio of rock images, ancient, stretched.
A live Navajo body, land, vault.

A camera eye opened to earth's fold and age.
Terra wrinklings, magma stretch-marks.

You hear windstorm, swirl, as you look.
Landscapes pottered into form.

The *White House* ruin takes you into time.
Under the roof as it were of chiseled overhang.

Look, too, at those saucer formations.
Petrified circle, disk, vortex.

Eyes up-point to hovering rock steps.
Bastion solids, unmovable.

The camera does heroic sweep.
A black and white visual liturgy.

Back to Back:
Man Ray, Horst P. Horst

Le Violon d'Ingres

I do not photograph nature. I photograph my visions.
　　　　　　—Man Ray

You think you know that back.
That beauteous back.
Was there a time you didn't see it?

You know it's Kiki de Montparnasse, model.
The turban, the twin f-holes, are familiar.
Lover but also instrument.

You know about Ingres, his violin.
French holds the title in idiom.
Hobby, pastime, *passe-temps.*

You know Ingres's nudes.
Classic languor. Women in repose.
The route to Kiki.

You know Ray's "All New York is Dada"
Yet always the American in Paris.
Duchamp, Lee Miller, Picabia, all weigh

You know the photograms, the rayographs.
Add in the portraits, the collage, the films.
His apertures into the surreal.

Do you then know *Le Violon?*
The disrobe, the withheld arms.
The turned head, the lash, the earring.

Do you then know the tease?
The real or playtime erotic.
Your own front to back gaze.

Mainbocher Corset

I am taking photographs because I like life.
      — Horst P. Horst

You think you know those *Vogue* images.
Fashion photography.
Cover glamour. Studio beauty.

You know Horst's high society eye.
Those perfect arcs of line and shade.
Gown and town, the cocktail hour.
You know Horst's Marlene and Coco.
His Dalí and Coward. The Windsors.
The celebrity elegances of couture.

You know the circuit.
Beaton to Avedon, Vreeland to Madonna.
Garment, pose, camp.

You know the nudes.
The gay-Greek legacy of classic body.
Add in the landscapes, Syria to Paris.

Do you then know that Venus back?
Its unlaced corset an erotic spinal cord.
Satin, hanging straps, the just about petticoat.

Do you then detect a mystery?
The desiring eye, the bound beauty.
Your own front to back gaze.

Sebastião Salgado: "Genesis"

My love letter to the planet.

—Sebastião Salgado

i.

Eight years to make, two hundred and more images.
The camera's sweep of vision, its illuminating aperture.
Monumental black and white, the command of monochrome.
Epic gaze under incorporating lens, closeness within distance.
For this is earth's scale and reach yet filled local presence.
Each image puts you amid hemispheres, congregations.
Perspectives of horizon and clime, land and sea.
The planet's residency, its light and shade breathings.

The sight-lines alone make you feel topographical.
Lava, berg, ocean, savannah, river, desert, jungle, sierra, ravine.
The vegetations alone make you feel organic.
Grassland, flora, leafage, tree, fern, bush.
The faces alone make you feel anthropological.
Indigene. Tribe. Nomad. Dynasty. Hunter. Womankind.
The wildlife alone make you feel fellow-inhabitant.
Sea mammal, reptile, simian, bird-flock, pachyderm, pod.

ii.

Visualities of polar ice, jungle, mountain.
Amazonia, El Pantanal, in verdure, lagoon and tree.
South Shetland of frozen arch and sculpture.
Congo vine lushly branched and curled.
Alaska glacier serrated, folded into sheet and cave.
Arizona canyon stretch-marked by wind and wet.
Arctic airflow of Baffin Island, Nunavut archipelago.
Africa heat-haze of Kalahari, Congo, Ruanda, Uganda.

Visualities of arboreal and plant life.
Tamarinds all upward-size, fruit and flower.
Grandidier Baobab, its trunk-bulb and medicine bark.
Helicopter maple tree in full greenery.
Cliff shrub, tundra moss, rainforest lichen, ancient pine.
Giant bladder kelp. Coral-floor forests.
Anchiote blooms all tropical dye and female bower.
Leaf and branch canopies of Madagascar.

Visualities of human face and body.
Papua's Yali, Sudan's Dinka, Brazil's Zo'é.
Navajo and Batak.
Firemakers. Herdsmen. Weavers.
Bangled brides-to-be. Chalked men dancers.
Boys in front of cacti. Girl tea worker.
Forest spearsmen. Fisher netsmen. Tree climbers.
Live clan, live progeny.

Visualities of kingdom'd animal.
Chinstrap penguins mass the Antarctic like wardens.
Alaska porcupine caribou hoof their trail.
Caiman gather in horizontal prowler appetite. Dolphins leap.
Blue footed boobie colonies nest. Buffalo and zebra raise dust.
Elephant seal crooks neck. Marine iguana lie rock-face still.
Mount Bisoke guerrilla hunches. The anhinga beaks its fish.
Galápagos turtle edges forward. Botswana giraffes give silhouette.

iii.

Eco-politics press for sure. Save the earth.
But this is planet-watch under camera art.
Continent. Hemisphere. Animalia. Visage.
An image lingers: that eye of southern Right Whale.
Cetacean telescope. Leviathan microscope.
Sea cornea, pupil, retina, gaze, across the panorama.
Nature's lens. Photography's optics.
Virtuoso seeing, whale, Salgado, and so ours.

Weegee: "My Man"

Street photographer? You bet.
Manhattan's camera Bogey.
Nighthawk shots.
Always right on the spot.
Ouija-uncanny.

Death. Blood. Brawl.
Burglaries and accidents.
Bowery calamities.
Shoot-up. Murder.
Life cuts.

My Man.
Dead on.
Dead (or dying) actually.
Shirt stained.
Unbuckled trousers.
Big sleep posture.

A woman's grief.
Her man-baby lapped.
Legs splayed. Urged to let go.
Tears of brute separation.
Farewell my lovely.

Weegee's camera his eye.
Ground level.
Sudden, beyond filter.
The seized, unglamorous moment.
Shoot!

Andre Kertesz:
"Broken Bench, New York"

I paint with light.
—Andre Kertesz

Quite a camera generation you have to say.
Hungary's own and then not.
Brassai, Moholy-Nagy, Kertesz.

Each Kertesz the observed accidental.
The limpid-clear image of un-perfection.
Fresh, a disjuncture, the eye gently surprised.

In *Broken Bench* there's the coated watcher.
You, yourself, as it were, also in the park.
Looking on, trying to see the whole.

The seated companion women.
The edge-side parked cars.
The lawn, leafed trees, bush gatherings.

And that foreground bench, half-damaged.
Situated as though awkward, its back slats askew.
A day-out's order casually unhinged.

The horizontals fallen into angle.
Slipped discs, loose shingles.
Wood and metal start-of-divorce proceedings.

The image has its tactics, its dare.
A bench brazenly severed.
Take me as you find me.

Robert Mapplethorpe's Body Culture

I see things as if they were sculptures

—Robert Mapplethorpe

Musculatures, black and white.
The photography of physique and pose.
Anatomy, male and female.
The photography of gaze and desire.

You could start with Charles Bowman.
Black torso, muscle, pubis.
You could start with Lisa Lyon.
Iron pumped womanhood.

There's Patti Smith.
Folded next to radiator.
There's Burroughs in tux as though at prayer.
Or Louise Bourgeois tumbling, Grace Jones staring.

Take a look at Warhol.
He might be hair-startled, the face neurasthenic.
Add in Philip Glass, Keith Haring, Philip Johnson.
The American arts in companion portrait.

The eye turns to Mapplethorpe himself.
Leather boy pose. Gangster pose. Camp pose.
Or self-bondaged. Anally bull-whipped.
Or full-faced, full of unblinking return stare.

Yes there are the flowers,
Narcissi. Orchids and lilies. Aptly.

But most you're amid bodies.
The sculptures of statuary and live flesh.

The Perfect Moment. Artist Rooms,
The controversies stirred.
Shock, horror, the homoerotic.
Bans, censorship, sexuality.

But always the un-censoring camera.
Studio black and white.
Bodies classic and sexual.
His bodies.

Diane Arbus:
"Patriotic Young Man
with a Flag"

Yes, human oddity.
But not without sympathy.
The portfolio lets you pick and choose.
The tattooed, the lipsticked, the wrinkled.
Dwarf to giant. Circus to food counter.
The unclothed, the differently sexual.
The just coiffured, the rococo behatted.
The unclad. The body-built.
The photographer herself, mirrored, auto-watchful.
Reportorial? Hardly.
Displacements seen each in their image.

1967 and the *Young Man*.

Euphoric, eyes raised.
Lapel patriot flag-badge.
Furled stars and stripes in hand.
"I'm Proud."

Pocked, drooping hair strand.
Shimmer shirt.
Hint of black under-vest.
"I'm Proud".

You have to think he is.
No worries, no complications.
Stark as the wall backdrop.

The hint of a smile.
Flag first.
Dangerous lucidity?

Beyond Vietnam, Civil Rights.
My Country 'Tis of Thee – and me.
What 1960s?

He worried Arbus didn't he?
He could worry you.
He could worry me.
He does.

David Bailey: "Kray Twins"

David bleedin' Bailey.
Blimey, London's East End.
Blimey, the Sixties.
Jagger, mini-skirts, Carnaby.
Sex, drugs, and you know what.
Shrimpton, Deneuve.
Even his own bloody film.
Blow-up. Not to say *Vogue* and its covers.
Alice Cooper snake-wrapped.

Swinging London?
Him and Duffy and Donovan.
Clicking its every trill and glitter.
Record sleeves, each Sunday paper.
British Pop Goes the Weasel.
Eventually the National Gallery.
Cheeky bugger.

Gloss books upon books.
Not least *Art of Violence.*
Its twin center the Krays.
Suited menace. Gangster glitz.
East's dockland to West End club-land.
Protection racket, gang-turf.
Boxing nights, pub knife or gun.
Sure, Python's Piranha Brothers.
Sure, Kemp twins playing Kray twins.
But also cockney-real villains.
Ronnie, insane, bisexual.
Reggie, knifer of Jack "The Hat" McVitie.
Ronnie and Reggie and mother Violet.
Complexities. Threat.

So you look close at the portrait.
The one face at the shoulder of the other.
Smart tailoring. Strangler tie-knots.
No could have been a contender regret.
Duck and dive street-savvy.
With killer punches.
Stares full of shoulder weight.
Compelling, soulless, un-regarding.

If not Ronnie, then Reggie
You're in for it.

Bailey's Own.

Andy Sotiriou: "Snowscapes"

A season, a series.
Snow highways.
Stillness, yes, or so it seems.
White drifts and edges.
Rock gatherings.
Tree vein and artery.
Leaf fringes.
Cloud passersby.
Stillness, yes, but not as it seems.

Each image a dynamic stillness.
Snow pile.
Silhouette white horizon.
Military telegraph poles.
Ski lift chessboard.
Cypress tree hang.
Shrub cul-de- sac.
Line drawing fence.

Live action.
Piled snowfalls.
Pathway curve.
Jigsaw bird-crowd.
Cruising pond swan.
Horizon snow walker.
Lone pedaling cyclist.
Hanging false pepper tree.

The images stare back.
Snow energy.
Speaking silence.
Two with colour messages.
Hillock, ice, flake.
Sky, chill, owl flight.
Weather geometry.
Haiku winter.

film

Film is a disease.

—Frank Capra

Silent Eruption: "Metropolis"

Phew.

Fritz Lang cinema to the brim.
Machine-future city of aboves and belows.
Religio-revolutionary epic.
Hell and Eden. Fire and Water.

You reach for every cavil.
Over the top screen opera. Bible allegory.
Plotline a zig, then zag, of crime and punishment.
Scenes and fades. Chases at speed.
Face and gesture straight from stage melodrama.
And, *longueurs*, your eye to the reel for two and a half hours.

German phrases indeed beckon.
Götterdämmerung. Sturm und Drang.
Or almost.

You have a killing player-cast.
Grim mogul father and road to Damascus son.
Heroine Holy Mary and Babylon Whore.
Mad god-scientist of cellar and clone.
Dragooned proles, nightclub tux and gown decadents.
Villain apparatchik.

Visions of Moloch. Tower of Babel image.
Dream, hallucination.
Ingredients the menu of near film disaster.

But then it's that classic status.
1926 cinema pioneer genius.

Expressionism. Art Deco. Dream.
Solid and shadow. Penthouse and catacomb.

That Manhattanesque vista.
Flying machine, sky-height train, bridge in air.
That underworld dystopia.
Dynamo, cog, electricity, dial.

That montage of lines and circles.
Worker columns, child crowds.
That collage all overlap and motif.
Face, dance, clock, stairway, elevator.

You think Murnau. You think Eisenstein.
Schreck's wall shadow Dracula.
Potemkin's Cossacks at the Odessa Steps.
And give your phew to *Metropolis*.

End of the Pier: "Brighton Rock"

Attenborough's Pinkie Brown.
Baby face. Empty of eye.
The mesh of his own cat's cradle.
No drink, no tobacco, no love.
The stare and threat of pathology.
The purest figuring of seaside ill.

Postwar England.
Tunnel of Fun. Petty gangland.
Song and dance. Villain razor.
Rose's trust. Pinkie's snarl.
Day out and deckchair fun.
Hell and "nor am I out of it."

You watch the threads of murder.
Funfair killing. Balcony push.
You watch the edge of comedy.
Ida's spirit-sleuth detection. Sergeant Plod.
You watch street to racetrack to suicide pact.
The last jump into Lethe black waters.

Boulting's guiding camera.
Green's rosary Catholicism.
Pinkie the counter-priest
Rose the sacrificial Mary.
World or church.
Whose precept rules?

The screen fills with geometries.
Beach chorus. Mob fight.
Hotel de luxe. Racket pay-up.
Goodtime pub. Shoddy hide-out.
Split love and hate voice recording.
Pier pleasure. Pier darkness.

Ozu's Ache of Intimacy:
"Tokyo Story"

Title kanji written on plain weave or burlap.
Tokyo Monogatari.
You enter the pace. Exact, deliberate, lyric.
Unrushed camera. Horizontal, face-on, memorial.
1950s black and white meticulous.

Inland Sea Onomichi to Tokyo Station.
Water's edge vista to belching chimney.
Garden plant to hanging laundry.
Children skyline running seen through age.
Lost horizons.

Hirayama family un-family.
Wanting parents, un-wanting offspring.
"We're here at last."
Journey from time as place.
Suburbs of being.

Pediatrician son. Beauty salon daughter.
Clerk son. Schoolteacher daughter.
Lost war son.
Shūkichi and Tomi mixed-fare marriage.
A dynasty of averages.

And Noriko, widow daughter-in-law.
Counter to insouciance, pettiness, drink.
The better self.
The keeper of time.
 Human heart but full of loss.

Brat children, spa noise.
Dizziness, coma, death.
The loudness of things said.
The loudness of things unsaid.
Ozu's film poem.

A. Robert Lee

Inside Space:
"Forbidden Planet"

Cinemascope. Eastmancolor.
Bubbles of electronic music.
Saucer craft. Hyper-light speed.
Not bad for a 23rd Century image.

You get no prizes for the Shakespeare.
Morbius as unwitting bad Prospero.
Altaira the space-princess Miranda.
Robbie a fond tin-man Caliban.

Jung you know enough to recognize.
Creature-wraith as Id.
The psyche undone by itself.
Attacks of invisibility and footprint.

It might be early *Star Trek.*
Valiant captain and crew.
Beam, astrogater, lost colony.
You've also got the race ancients of Krell.

There's creak and groan.
Sets of painted sky and desert.
Hollywood costume and kiss.
A hint of Yellow Brick Road.

But the fable's screening has its wins.
Cubist dynamo. Art Deco dial.
Plotline hieroglyphics of omnipower.
The competing planets of mind.

Pioneer in all senses.
Cinema of early stellar magic.
Voyage, suspense, science.
Space, outer and inner.

Civilization and Its Discontents: "Queimada"

Slash and burn.
The Lower Antilles.
Sugar cane colony.
Portuguese 1840s.
But transferably Spanish, English, French.

Pontecorvo Cinecittà parable.
Full red screen opening.
Morricone "Abolição" soundtrack.
Raptor flights.
Toussaint allusions.

The plot itself a plot.
Slave lines, chains, freedom, dream.
Brando in William Walker fop-English.
José Dolores as history's emissary.
Servants of two masters.

The moment's regime change.
A one language, a one uniform.
Sugar in your tea.
Stock exchange.
Fire, bullet, garrote, gallows.

"You can't kill a myth."
The secret agent revealed.
Dolores's death for life.
No more token bread.
No more whisky for rum.

Colonialism's burnt out case.
"Your bag Sir."
White baggage.
Black porterage.
The knife-stab into freedom.

Film Art: "Barry Lyndon"

It's painterly, a canvas, Irish green, English landscape, you hear said.
It's literary, Parts 1 and 2, picaresque, a poem, you hear said.
It's orchestral, a music, scores, too, by Schubert, Vivaldi, you hear said.
But, most, it's best cinema, Kubrick triumph, you hear yourself say.

It may be you'll do duty by Thackeray and the novel.
You can dip into history, Seven Years War, Georgian England.
There's Great Estate fortune, etiquette and gaming, a widow.
But, most, it's the camera eye, its measure, its precision.

Lyndon's rise and fall may well be Cautionary Tale.
Irish farm boy to English gent, cottage to mansion.
The incarnations come and go: soldier, spy, husband, rake, lost father.
But, most it's screen rhythm, exactness, image for image.

You travel with the film, Dublin to Holland, Belgium to Prussia.
But each stop a portrait, a call to sight and prospect.
Landscape tree and cloud, recruitment, soldier line, gaming cheat and table.
But, most, the final duel, a theatre of bullet and wound.

A narrator gives laconic story-line, a voice, an ear, to seeing.
You have an intermission to take stock, ponder progress.
Death of a child, the revenge of a stepson, the loss of a leg.
But, most, the directing baton, the power of composition.

Other Kubrick seizes, earns its keep.
Plunge into dystopia with *Orange*, enter space with *2001*.
Find blood, haunt, and history in *The Shining*.
But, most, be absorbed by *Lyndon's* magic aperture.

Shadow Life: "Touch of Evil"

Welles of course.
Hank Quinlan.
Bulk, sweat, grunt, cigar.
And cane.
Candy bar and strangulation.
True and fixed justice.
"He was some kind of man".

Juncture and disjuncture.
Talk Mexican. Talk American.
Talk Vargas and Suzie.
Fiesta and threat.
Blonde Leigh. Gypsy Marlene.
Blur of good-bad cop.
Detections.

Crepuscular. Night vision.
Opening track. Bomb. Arrest.
Dynamite, drug, motel, cell.
Pumping oil rig.
Bridge stalk and tape.
Shots in the night.
Black death-water pool.

Always that director genius.
Hank's gross, eye-weary face.
Body weight as moral glut.
Always the lens of street, below-street.
Grandi clan. Right about Sanchez.
Shoebox clue.
"My dirty job."

Camera at ground level and slant.
Aperture narrowed.
Shaded frame for frame.
Car, doorway, balcony.
Gang, chase, desert, jukebox.
Kafka hall of records.
Darkest pursuits.

What but crime and punishment?
What but border noir?
The whole ambiguous reel.

Frontier Score:
"Once Upon a Time in the West"

It may be the opening silence and wait.
Jack Elam gun-barrel trapping the fly.
Woody Strode hat-catching the water drip.
The twitch of their ill-faced companion.
The chug, the hiss, the whistle of the Iron Horse.
And then Charles Bronson "Harmonica."
Alone, one against three, granite.
Duel. Gunshot. More silence.
A Prologue, a myth of frontier, to savor.

The plot unfolds: a tale of retribution.
Banditry, train, frontier, township.
Pistol lean Henry Fonda.
Widow beauty Claudia Cardinale.
Gunslinger worn unshavenness Jason Robards.
And always, eyes fixed, revenge-in-person Bronson.

C'era una volta il West
Sergio Leone's camera.
American West, Italy in Almería.
The final shoot-out.
Harmonica and recognition.
Final sunset ride-away.

C'era una volta il West
Ennio Morricone's music.
Perfect music to haunt.
Echoic, strange, compelling.
Frontier sound on silence.
The West's own mythic score.

Goddam: Nina Simone's "Montreux 1976"

Documentary? Kind of.
You watch almost as much as you listen.
There's something tense, spiky, about Nina.
You wouldn't dare to think "entertainment."
The accusing stare, the mouth, the teeth.
You are on notice, jazz-blues as rebuke.
It's talking song.
Anthem, sermon.
Mourning. Race. Anger. Sadness.
With Bach behind the dazzling piano work.
A wondrous musical discomfort.
"Sit down girl, sit down."
The growl from the piano stool.
"Feeble."
Her word to Swiss-white listeners
after the call to co-sing the ballad.

Enter with "Little Girl Blue."
Pause, silence, lyric.
"What can you do...
liberated little girl blue?"
As always the piano.
Its rolls, flights, excursions.
"I talk a lot...I don't give a damn."
She says before "Backlash Blues."
Words from Langston Hughes.
"I know how hard it's been for you."
Then "Be My Husband."
Love-call, regret, black Piaf.
Or rather just Simone.

"We always have a story."
The way into "Feelings."
"Nothing more than feelings."
Selma. Birmingham. Martin.
Voice, piano, full of saturated history.
"Goddam, what a shame
we have to write a song like that."
No mere performance this.
Viscera. Pulse. Contemplation.
Fugue ending.

Who do you think of?
Billy, Janice, Gwendolyn, Ai.
But Simone ever, always,
in her own right.
Dangerous sounding
      On her own screen.

Cello Music: "Departures"

Yojiro Takita screen.
A choreography.
The haunt of passage.
Fog and rain.
Disbanded orchestra.
Comic entry into new employ.

That of *Okuribito.*
A sender-off. Encoffinment.
The translations waver.
Nōkan.
Passage of farewell.
Body dressed and flamed into afterlife.

Japan corpse taboo.
A ritual of cleansing.
Travel agency indeed.
Departures young, old, wrong gender.
Grief, anger: all religions.
Life ceremonies amid death.

The erotics of funeral couture.
Hometown of coffin and bathhouse.
Salmon dead and alive.
Geese flight.
Daigo father loss.
Mika new life.

Letter stones each its own connection.
Foodways of life, *Sasaki-sensei, Uemura-san.*
Brahms, Beethoven, Ave Maria.
Always the string and pitch of cello.
Childhood to childhood, death to death.
The camera's farewell music of one generation to another.

Exenomorph:
The "Alien" Chronicles

Alien
Body of slither, whiptail, glans-like head.
Dripping saliva'd teeth row.
Acid-pure blood.

That squid-claw burst from Kane's chest.
Those heaves of birth cones.
The gelatinous cocoon pods.

Flamethrower, airlock.
Crew expendable.
Ash's robot fracture, brain milk.

Nostromo, Narcissus.
But also the Conrad of *Heart of Darkness*.
Count-down to detonation.

Feline Jones. Serpent alien.
Shuttle hatch.
Hypersleep.

Last survivor of the *Nostromo*.
Signing Off. Crusoe.
Long Day's Journey into Night.

Aliens
Return to planetoid LV-426.
Corporation.
Multimillion-dollar installation.

"Express elevator to hell."
Top Gun Marine.
Bishop android.

Secretion. Drip.
Acid holes. Hive.
Nightmare pursuit.

"You bitch" mother of species.
Ripley in Class 2 Loader.
Gladiators.

Newt the girl survivor.
Shared last exit.
Sleep flight.

Alien 3
Prison-refinery planet.
YY chromosome criminals.
Millenial godhead.

Weyland-Yutani corporation.
Profit and weapon.
Killer specimen.

Incisor and tail pursuit.
Flight, speed.
Huis clos.

Ripley and enchested alien.
Hatchling queen.
Molten furnace double end.

Alien: Resurrection
Two centuries necromancy.

DNA war science.
Ripley clone-daughter.

Dystopian perfection.
Assassin diabola.
Death's doppelganger.

Hybrid offspring expulsion.
Earth vista.
Back to the future.

Alien Chronicle
Director fiat.
Scott. Cameron. Fincher. Jeunet.
H.R. Giger bio-vampire design.

Flight. Haunt. Fear.
Dark-ways space.
Alien shadow.

Ship and planet.
Prison and lab.
Alien life.

AVP hunter spin-offs.
Prometheus "creation" prequel.
Alien continuance.

Minutes to go.

A Rufus Over Your Head:
"Duck Soup"

For Jared Lubarsky

"Join the Army and see the Navy"
Ducks in a pot. Groucho's tash. Harpo's scissors.

"Who you gonna believe, you or your own eyes?"
Freedonia: you know it's the promise of madcap.

"A gala day for you."
Trumpets, chorus, wardrobe, entrance down the firepole.

"Oh, Your Excellency!" "You're not so bad yourself."
Spoof love talk. Aim and fire insult.

"How about taking up the tax?" "How about taking up the carpet?"
Politics-speak slap. Bureaucrat-authority slap.

"All God's chillun got guns."
Spiritual turned to war.

Scene for scene it's cartoon, fade, turvy.
Firefly wooing. Mrs. Teasdale braying.
Chico/Harpo anti-spy pair. Vera's Latin-slink Mata Hari.
Lemonade and peanut vaudeville with hat routine.
Doorway sight gag. Silent mirror nightshirt pantomime.
Treason trial by elephant joke.
Mass rush to the front, fire engines to porpoises.
Groucho festooned in successive military garb.
Victory pelting by apple, orange and tomato.

No doubting the targets.
Tinpot authority, petty rank, battle fever.
You think of the generation's cine-galaxy.
Chaplin, Keaton, Lloyd, Stan and Ollie, Fields, Mae West.
But still it's Groucho, and brothers all.
Style, speed, quippery.
Black and white screen turns.
Golden wit and acrobatics.
A thousand stirs to laughter.

Sculpture

Sculpture is the art of the hole and the lump.

—Auguste Rodin

Parthenon

Ο Παρθενώνας.
Ο *parthenonas*.
Parthenon Marbles.
And yes, you could say, the Elgin Marbles.

The Parthenon.
History takes you back to templed Athena.
Then to Greek Church and Turkish Mosque.
And even to Gunpowder Store.
You remember Empires.
Byzantine. Ottoman. Venetian. British.

Since Elgin, the English 7th Earl, the sites divide.
Disputes, wars of possession and word.
Byron gave his smack as did Mercouri.
Doric splendor. Colonial theft.
Classic Greece. Larcenous Albion.
Acropolis and British Museum.

You let this somehow inhabit the art.
But not rule it.

Athens frieze.
Gods. Polis. Family.
Male cavalry. Female weavers.
Ceremony and Procession.
Rites and Sacrifice.
Ritual more lost than found.

Athens sculptings.
Perfect Selene horse-head, battling centaur.

Dionysos handsomely at rest, warrior horsemen.
Helios rising, draped sister goddesses.

Compositional, inter-positioned.
Anatomies from life and size.
Olympic, too, ideal, deific.
Time's gift, time's beauty.

You see it even in broken statuary.
You see it even in broken ownership.

Pole Position

The very names carve a poetry.
Kwakiutl, Haida, Tlingit, Nootka.
First nations of word and meaning.
Another language.
For Pacifica. The Northwest. Alaska.

You could say symbol or decoration.
But you know the risk of tourist-speak.
Memory, rather, of clan and lineage.
Red cedar semaphore.
Designs of realm and story.

Thunderbird wings spread wide.
Raven beak, whale head.
Bear, otter, salmon, eagle.
Beaked faces. Outstretched tongues.
Native chisel.

Learn the grammar.
Welcome, death, memory.
Shaman fare. Even tease.
High to lowest on the totem pole.
Each, new and ancient, a calling card.

Step into Native timeline.
Give sight to trunk, gauge, dye.
Savor heraldry's carve and craft.
Alert Bay or Howkan.
You have the privilege of invitation.

Stones and Peace: "Noguchi in Paris"

i.

Landscape. Garden. Sculpture.
The overlap teases even as it holds you.
Is this UNESCO France or UNESCO Japan?
The eye, imbibing, says both, and then more.

Sakura, plum tree and bamboo.
Lake ripple, gurgle stream, fall of water.
Cross the Hiroshige bridge, regard the lotus floats.
Tantric, a calligraphy of peace, *wā.*

Circles of raked pebble.
Pathways under eastern pergola.
Banks reflected in pool shimmer.
Paving as hand-drawn as *kanji.*

ii.

Stones, earth's own sculpting, act to mark and pivot.
Axis and satellite, uprights and flats.
The perfect pattern amid flower and cascade.
Each a weather, an archive.

Time stones, stepping stones.
Heart stones, head stones.
They speak loud silence.
Shapings of space and spirit.

Blue-grey, rust, lichened or not.
They secure the garden's design.
Codes, a Japanese language.
Noguchi's sentinels for peace.

Rodin Live

Les Bourgeois de Calais.
The eye looks upon them in different loci.
France, for sure, but Philadelphia and Copenhagen.
It also looks upon different histories.
English feudal conquest. Hundred Years War.
Burghers, the six of them.
Un-shoed, bare of head, noosed, bearers of keys to the city.
Shapes of anguished surrender.

Sculpture as dirge, fate, bronze elegy.
In one sense how un-spectacular.
Together yet separate, scapegoats marked for sacrifice.
You see anguish, query, above all a pending.
You look upon gaze turned in upon itself.
The sculptor's hand shapes each body's feeling.
A fashioning of shared aloneness.
The reverse of ceremony.

For sure there's other Rodin.
The Kiss, he knows life's kinetics.
Turn to *John the Baptist,* all force of prophecy.
Admire his *Thinker,* the anatomy of concentration.
Summon Dante and the *Gates of Hell.*
Stride alongside his *Walking Man.*
Face robed *Balzac,* sea-edged *Hugo.*
Seize the real of *The Age of Bronze.*

Then return to *The Burghers of Calais.*
Not Greece nor Renaissance this.
Neither *Venus de Milo* nor Michelangelo's *David.*
These are the physiques of modernity.

Beings inhabited, breathed, blooded.
Their fear, their self-contemplation.
Sad, plinthed in fate as in sculpture.
Rodin's sculpting of life at death's shadow.

After Flight:
Alexander Calder's "Flamingo"

i.
Steel red. Calder red.
His *stabile* triumph.

What perfect sculpture-size.
Arch high, abstract.

Chicago's West Adams Federal Plaza.
Mies van der Rohe dark office frame.

Open monument, curvilinear.
Flamingo, city, walker.

ii.
Nature's stately migrant.
Feather and limb.

Leg braced, wing spanned.
Neck bent, beak a filter.

Folded plume.
Landed, wading.

Vermilion to the eye.
Colour coded.

iii.
You become art's ornithologist.
Witness to the magic of air to ground.

You take in the respite from flight.
The sculptor's seizure of Nature's form.

You see and return to see.
Bird majesty. Art's hand.

You look straight, around, and up.
The descent Calder brings from the skies.

Attenuating Circumstance:
Alberto Giacometti

A lifetime of Swiss diligence.
Appropriately clinical, dark.
Creativities of bust, mask, graphic.
And sexual, the voyeur's lure.
Wasn't he, too, an era's denizen of the surreal?
Didn't he, too, sign on to Sartre's existential register?
Later Giacometti would compose no one else's signature.

An abundance.
Watercolour, Diego brother's head.
Landscape, sketch, illustrated page.
Miniatures to life size, even solids.

But what you go on seeing is the figure in space.
Men, women, ambient, or pointing, or spoon-like.
Winnowed, thinned, the body as vertical, a filament.

The forward incline of *L'Homme Qui Marche 1*.
A striding man of true height and arm, humanity.
The emaciated selfhood of *Femme Debout*.
A standing woman, fragile, vulnerability.
The fivesome of *La Place*.
A city square of *piétons* each their shadow.
The Cleopatra rider and wheels of *Le Chariot*.
A vehicling, a balance, of time and motion.

Bronze or plaster the idiom beckons.
Beckett for his set, Genet for his text.
Sculpture's call to core, the distilled.
An un-encumbrance you think you recognize.
Marrow as it were.

Reclining with Henry Moore

i.
Almost a horizontal lifetime.
I mean looking sideways-on.
Figure upon figure in repose.
As if the sculpture needed a bed-partner.

Not to say there aren't uprights.
Family group, miners, wartime Tube Londoners.
But you revisit Moore's reclining figures.
Organic bronze or stone or wood.

Abstraction of torso, limb.
Curvature of spine, hip, pelvis.
Fluidity of womb or breast.
The natural form a wave, a music.

ii.
Draped Seated Woman.
Propped, leg and thigh approaching you.
Draped Reclining Woman.
One arm holding the proportion of body.

Draped Reclining Mother and Child.
Maternity's love.
Ample, enclosing.
A circle of birth and body.

Fitzwilliam Museum Reclining Figure.
Actively supine.
Whited. Shadowed.
Hollowed out. Full.

Louise Bourgeois: "Maman"

The spider is an ode to my mother...Like the spider, my mother was a weaver.

—Louise Bourgeois

Arachnid giant poise.
Eight spindle leg arches.
Bronze-bulb abdomen and thorax.
Twenty-plus marble eggs.
Motherly in torqued steel.

A comfort? Some speak of protectress.
Female principle, fecundity.
A threat? Some speak of devouress.
Bite, sting, threat, dream.

Try others.
Weaver-god.
Tapestry maker.
Guardian of labyrinths.
Web queen.

Whichever, each, this is insect majesty.
Regnant in height and station.
No cobweb bother, mere irritant.
Rather giant harmonium.

Sculptured for dynamic scuttle.
Sculptured for womb, for birth.
Sculptured for nurture, for life.
Sculptured for art's own weave.

Niki de Saint Phalle:
"Miss Black Power"

Hakone's Open Air Museum.
A train hour and whistle from Tokyo.
Lake and mountain, Picasso and Moore.

And Saint Phalle.
You can track the sculptor's life.
French birth, American family.
Paris and Mallorca.
Model, marriages, California.
Gaudí and Dalí, Tinguely, Tarot.
And each lavish doll-figure.
A bravura of form, coloration.

Miss Black Power.
Her one of many giant women.
Africa body, squared shoulders.
Egyptian pillar legs.
Circle painted target breasts.
Miró-veined coat of colours.
Blue bag clasped in hand.
Black gynocentric strength.

Here and now woman.
Here in Japan woman.
Here in America woman.
Here in the world woman.

Monumental, feet planted.
Afro-America.
IN YOUR FACE.

Whale Paths: Frank Stella and "Moby Dick"

Once the planes begin to bend and curve and deform then you get into what happens in "Moby Dick."

—Frank Stella

The labels have their place.
Abstract impressionist, the postmodern.
Influences invite note.
Russia's Lissitzky and Kandinsky, Picasso.
Avant-garde? Utterly, a vision storm.

But given these nods Stella has his own eye.
Melville's epic in two-hundred-plus constructions.
Worked aluminum torque. Magnesium curve.
Beluga reliefs, sculptures, castings, each gyre and guttering.
An 1850s text sighted, colour-vivid in 1980s re-seeing.

Start with *Loomings*, fashioned wave, a threading.
The imagining of voyage, whale, whiteness.
Take on *Spirit Spout* as if up-surged vapor.
Multi-colour, spectrum, spray and bulk.
Evanescence sculpted into solid.

You might enter *The Grand Armada.*
Birthing whales caught in surge, in billow.
Vivacity of paint, swirl of metal.
How not to sense Cetacean dynamo, ocean bulk?
Liquid domain of umbilical and whale.

One for one, Stella's own kabuki.
The Whiteness of the Whale, imaged un-colour.
Heads or Tails, helixed ends.

The Chase. Third Day, rendered battle and harpoon.
The Town Ho's Story, monumental twist of survival.

Ishmael or Ahab. Sphynx or Pipe.
Queequeg's coffin or Fedallah's secret.
Careful disorderliness said Melville.
Irregular shapes says Stella.
Worked oceans both. Art's seas of imagination.

China Dragon: Ai Weiwei's "S.A.C.R.E.D"

Some credential.
Ai Quing poet father. Lu Quing painter wife.
Red Guard Shihezi exile.
Beijing art and film avant-garde.
East Village decade English.
Activism and police beating.
China legacy honoured.
China under reprimand.

According to What: creation's multi-forms.
Bird's Nest: stadium controversy.
Fifth Avenue Pulitzer Fountain: ancient heads.
Sunflower Seeds: porcelain China craft.
Alcatraz Exhibition: Lego and dragon installed freedom.

Eyes art-wide.
Europe of Duchamp-surreal.
America fan, Warhol and Ginsberg.
Crab satire at Blenheim Palace.
Han dynasty coca-cola vase.
Brooklyn stacked bicycle cascade.

But always New China sculpture, creation.
But always Old China surveillance, de-creation.
Movement, arrest.
Photo-image, Manhattan books, record cover.
Internet, song.
Shanghai studio. Caochangdi studio.
Visual wit. Ironic code.
Political blackjack.

S.A.C.R.E.D.
Iron coffin cells, all six.
81 day-night detention.
Fiberglass real. Diorama crafted.
You peer, a Tom, a witness.
Supper, each swallow guard-watched,
Accusers, confession to what?
Cleansing, shower-nakedness, clothed soldiery.
Ritual, prison march-in.
Entropy, sheeted sleep under monitor.
Doubt, seated toilet reflection.

Regime un-freedom.
Imagination's democracy.

China dragon Weiwei.

Ron Mueck: Magnus

On the one hand, I try to create a believable presence, and on the other, they have to work as objects.

—Ron Mueck

i.
Dunno. You just keep looking.
Sheer size.
Magnified faces, torsos, skin.
Enhancement. Ogre-ish.
The enjoyable unease of threat.

You know it's fiberglass, silicone.
You know it's plaster, resin.
Yet each is hyper-simulacrum.
Scale, dimension, presses the impact.
Larger as further degree of real.

ii.
Try *Mask II,* likely his own face.
Sideways on, gargantuan.
Lids closed, lips thickly pursed.
Brow an artery, ear big, whiskers dotted.
Sleeping? A moment's defiant pause?

Try *A Girl,* newborn, skin-knotted.
Frowning. Tight of eye.
Wrinkled. Veins lightly close to surface.
Hair amniotically damp.
Just delivered.

Try *Two Women.*
Coated, slippered, a paired huddle.

Folded arms, shoulders bent, the stare.
Who you looking at?
Mind your own business.

Try *A Man in a Boat.*
In the buff.
Arms folded.
Not even rowing.
Just cross-legged, looking out.

Try *In Bed.*
Her elbow crooked.
Hand to face, knees raised.
Propped, pillowed.
Gaze beckoned beyond the linen.

Try *Boy.*
Giant crouch.
Arms raised.
Trim back
Gymnastic stare.

iii.
Dunno. You just keep looking.
Sheer bigness.
But art, always, the eye's perspective.
Sculpture bravura.
Try Mueck for size.

Architecture

Every great architect is – necessarily – a great poet.

—Frank Lloyd Wright

London Transitions

i.
Burlington Arcade
Regency footsteps.
Lord Cavendish's covered arcade.
Make your entrance on to the red carpet.
Beadles either end.
Up-market roof above your head.

Regency comedy.
Why the enclosed corridor?
M'lord's anti-dumping.
Hoi-polloi rubbish.
Oyster shells into his garden.

Regency prices.
Antique, jewel, earring.
Cashmere, perfume, chocolate.
Silk jacket and Med-swimsuit.
"Rare and collectables."

Regency footfall.
Toff-wear window display.
Shoe polish service.
Time's vintage watches.
Gentility since 1819.

ii.
Albert Memorial
Wonderfully preposterous.
Victoria's Victoriana.
Gilbert Scott baroque.
Yet a regal widow's fond lament.

Gilt-bronze Albert.
Dead of typhoid's 1861 ravage.

Imperium stalks your way there.
Queen's Gate. Prince's Gate.
Prince Consort Road.
The Royal Albert Hall.
Imperial College.
And none other than the V&A.

Discrepancies enter.
Latter Day Saints Temple.
Sir Alexander Fleming Building.
The Proms with Land of Hope and Glory.
The busker guitaring Pachelbel.
The Royal Park with skateboarders.
Start with the plinth and then ascend.
Global queen astride the beasts.
The span of continents.
Europe. America. Asia. Africa.
Bull. Bison. Elephant. Camel.
And then the podium.

Master of the domains.
Manufactures. Horticulture.
Commerce. Engineering.
Sculptures of the Virtues.
Sculptures of the Arts, the Sciences.
Albert, plus angels, canopied under mosaic.

Posed, ornate, regnant.
Over a Parnassus frieze of hundreds.
Poetry to Science.
Sculpture to architecture.

Painting to Music.
Each the eye of imagination.

"Queen Victoria and Her People."
The age's Boadicea to her Consort.
The public good, tribute, memory.
How to doubt it? A worthy.
Albert as God-ordained Englishman.
Never mind the Saxe-Coburg accent.

iii.
Pancras Station
To wags, and those of uncertain English,
Saint Pancreas.
Dig into martyrology.
There's the beheaded Roman Christian convert.
But it's Gothic frontage, red brick and spires.
More Victoriana. Railway England.
So you remember the Barlow train shed.
The Grand Hotel. The Age of Steam.
Scott architecture once again. Solidity.
Now step into modernity.
Revival out of 1960s platform dank.
Betjeman campaign and commemoration in bronze.
His name an eatery of "Best of British Breakfasts."
Paul Day "Meeting Place," embrace, scale, cell phone.
The inset arch, the hanging multicolour panel.
Lower level arcade. Wine and "Order Food."
The Renaissance Hotel, stars and all.
As much day-out gallery as station.
Earlier travel becomes future travel.
Internet your ticket.
Pay by card.
Eurostar and International Departures.

Head at speed to Le Gare du Nord.
Select a silent carriage.
But take another look at driveway and storey.
Memory's concourse, clock tower, ceremony.
Victorianism on a time machine.

iv.
Gherkin
Now you're up to date.
Norman Foster's cross-hatch.
High-rise swirl.
Diamond windows.
Street triangle entries.
City of London business chic.
Swedish built—what else?—postmodern.

You can go formal.
Swiss Re Building.
30 St. Mary Axe.
Forty-one levels. Monied.
Fellow high-rises do duty.
The Shard as upward arrow.
Lloyds all Fritz Lang *Metropolis* towers.

You ponder the twist and shout.
Does working there lead to dizziness?
Suits, male, female, swan back and forth.
You see cleaners platform-swabbing the glass wrap.
Night-lit it might be an interstellar capsule.
Sky News, right titled, broadcasts.
London calling.

Prague Album

i.

Karluv Most
The Charles Bridge.
You start there, how could you not?
Prague's footfall artery.
Echoes over the cobbles.
Voices Czech, German, Hebrew and Yiddish.
Charles IV in Holy Roman Emperor garb.
Bohemians, Moravians, Silesians.
History behind the stones: Jan Hus, Thirty Years War.
Hitler tanks, Russia, Communism.
1968 Prague Spring and Dubček.
1989 Velvet revolution.
1993 Czechoslovakia, juncture and divorce.
Havel of word and presidency, airport and museum.
Vistas: castle, cathedral, monastery, national theatre.
Watch the night-lit wheel of gulls over the bridge tower.
See musician, sketcher, prostate beggar and dog, kiosk.
Contemplate the underflow and shimmer of the Vlatava.
Book a cruise on *Charm of Czechia* or *Grand Bohemia*.
But always you are back to the bridge.
Yourself time's latest cross-stroller, step and eye.
Arches, statued sainthoods, the baroque.
Stone weight, stone time passage.

ii.

Staromëstské námëstí
Old Town Square.
You think of others.
Brussels *Grand Place*. Madrid *Plaza Mayor*.
Few quite match the sighted bounty.
Medievalism's Astronomical Clock, chime and calendar.
Gothicism's Týn Church of Our Lady, tower upon tower.

Ceremony's Hus Memorial, epic, protestant.
Art's Kinský Palace, classic, stucco, roseate.
You flâneur the architecture: Nouveau. Deco. Cubist.
The restaurants advertise "Pork Knee, Prague Speciality."
The Square leads on and into the panorama.
The Jewish Cemetery like disheveled pages from the Torah.
The Kafka Museum the shadow of the author's claustrophobia.
The Castle complex the vaunt of state architecture, world heritage.
The St.Vitus Cathedral, its vaults God-high.
The tourist hum, musicians, the trolley clang.
Prague's inner self built out.

iii.
Strahovský klášter
Strahov Monastery.
Homework tells you it's *Premonstratensian.*
Home to the order of canons.
Twelfth century founded. Romanesque. Hussite-raided.
Basilica, stucco-white.
You make your way to the library halls.
Theological and Philosophical.
And via the discomforting Cabinet of Curiosities.
Formidable shelf rows under fresco ceilings.
Positioned atlas globes.
Bound manuscripts, a *bibliorum sacrorum.*
Scholar splendour, bible and science.
But then a moment's anarchy enters the mind.
Isn't this tourist fetish, a day-trip into the medieval?
Who reads these tomes, are they read?
Imagine a library card, a bar-code?
Wouldn't you like to browse, rip out a page?
Your malign thought gets duly chastised.
This is history's edifice.
Its monastery an art, its books a clock.

iv.
Fred and Ginger
Dancing House.
Prague Modern you think.
Or Prague Postmodern.
Gehry-Milunić design.
Riverfront corner torque.
Turquoise window.
Art salon gallery.
Bird's Nest restaurant.
A reworked Tower of Pisa.
Crushed coke-can say detractors.
Ballet glide say admirers.
Awkward bent elbow. Fine additional limb.
The summons of swing-time Hollywood.
Architecture's musical.
But also full of self-proclaiming now.
The city, they say, deconstructed.
Prague's call to new architectural eye.

Corner Spain

i.
Ciudad Encantada.
You're close to Cuenca.
Castilla-La Mancha.
Amid circled winter rocks.
Time and weather alphabet.

Each stone speaks its Spanish name.
El Puente. El Mar de Piedra. La Tortuga.
But your own eye does its imagining.
Face rock. Wind rock. Mushroom rock.
Cottage and roof. Tower and circle.

You see more at each gaze.
Thick cliff lips.
Great humpback flukes.
Boulder paired lovers.
Wailing walls.

Amble through snow-patched alleys.
Enter cretaceous mapping.
Think time whorls, place marks.
Measure Nature's architecture.
Relish Spain's magic geology.

ii.
Almería village.
One of a hundred.
Hillside slope.
Simple blue door.
White plaster wall.

Home entrance.
Barred window.
Timber studs.
Metal letterbox.
Meters gas and electric.

It's the blue that holds you.
Shadowed in the sun.
Noon sky or shimmer-sea.
Indigo, cobalt.
Miró pastel. Picasso brush.

Exact. Pigmented. Found.
Life and place framed.
Yes, a door.
Yes, a picture.
Spain's winning blue optic.

iii.

Navarra *sidrería*. Navarra *cidery*.
Village of Cizur Menor as against Cizur Mayor.
Or Zizur Txikia if, er, you're up on your Basque.

Brief hill drive from Pamplona.
La Cochera. Coach house.
Old-time for garage.
Tawny brick, door within door.

You face the cider barrel.
Huge, coopered from Brogdingnag.
Stave and tap.
A reservoir.

Each ladle pouring a ballet.
El Escanciado.

Aim. Arc. Glass.
And tapas of tortilla and olive.

Enter site, calendar.
Tradition both real and invented.
A building to speak custom.
Spain's food and drink parking.

iv.
Aeropuerto de Madrid-Barajas, now *Adolfo Suárez.*
Terminal Four. Rogers-Lamela design.
Sweep and nave.
Corridor of hub, light, gate.

You can think comparisons.
The ceiling moons of TWA Terminal at JFK.
Changi's giant-ant buttresses and carpet floor.
Beijing of the one overarch and skylight dots.

The eye alights on each double-fork support.
Yellow, green, blue.
The wave and curve of roof.
The hanging metal décor.

Daytime and it's a touch of the Beaubourg.
Night gives you lighting in satellite-dish glow.
Both yield tube, lattice, arcade.
Spain's new takeoff and land architecture.

Medieval New York

New York New York.
Manhattan city grid, matrix, hub.
Futurist, the modern.
Verticals, widths, avant-garde block.
High-rises the skyline of dream.
Bowery to 125th a Broadway of geometries.
Central Park as Olmsted's benign green lung
Brooklyn's bridge for Hart Crane's American harp.
The Chrysler flecked deco.
The Guggenheim's spiral, MOMA's holdings.
View Rothko, Pollock, Warhol.
Hear the jazz of Parker, Miles, Monk.
Take in John Cage music, Merce Cunningham dance.
Read Frank O'Hara, John Ashbery.
Watch *Manhattan* with an ear to Gershwin's "Rhapsody."
Sidestep the winter Metro steam.
Learn Avenue and Street, the Hudson and East rivers.
Flag a yellow cab.
Architectures of now.
New York's tradition of the new.

But then head further up-town, up-river.
Manhattan North, Fort Tryon Park.
1930s-opened. The Middle Ages borrowed.
Cloister re-makes, France to Catalonia.
Museology of edifice, garden, tower.
Art's medieval passageways.
Churchly, pietistic.
Sculpture, tapestry, stained glass, manuscript.
Dutch unicorn weaving, Romanesque cross.
Altar piece and illuminated book.

Herb planting, chapel artifact.
Pillar and shaded courtyard.
All yours up by the Palisades.
A Train to 190th with bus to follow.
Ride into history, park if you choose.
Tickets into time.
Architectures of then.
New York's new of tradition.

Chicago Stock

i.
The Hancock.
You see it at a distance.
Presiding against Lake Michigan.
Tall enough, two ant horn antennae.
Skyline emblem to the city.

Make your top deck observation.
Eye Wrigley and fellow high-rises.
Survey the Loop.
Trace Chicago River, Lakeshore Drive.
Agree, or not, to the Magnificent Mile.

You think the address just right.
North Michigan Avenue.
The hues look modest.
Granite-black, shadow grey.
Like a sensible coat.

Cross-braced façade.
X's against upright.
Plaza base. Waterfall. Height.
No wonder the fond label.
Big John.

ii.
Cabrini Green.
White Italian. Black poor.
Sainthood named. Tenant lived.
Poverty. Gang, Violence. Drugs.
City blight.
History's damp.

Loss yet vital community.
The Projects.

Cabrini Green.
Near North Side.
1940s to modern demolition.
Vandal. Cockroach, Graffiti.
City block.
History's cells.
Public housing yet vital private life.
The Projects.

iii.
Emil Bach House
Hard not to see the irony.
Frank Lloyd Wright.
Rogers Park.
Prairie style in the suburb.
Cube geometry.
Double storey.
Slab roofing.
Apron veranda.
Sand coloration.

Sheridan Road monument.
Room of insets, designed squares.
Wedged, exact furnishing.
Fire hearth.
Boxed light.

iv.
The L.
It starts with spelling.
L, "L," EL, "El."
Each makes its bow.

Learn CTA Lines.
Red, Green, Orange.
Not to mention Brown, Pink, Purple.
Each the index of neighbourhood.

Look up, hear the clank, the rail creak.
Watch train aerials: line and T-Junction.
Dip, steer, beneath each metal arch.
Head down into subway.

Iron rail lattice amid the high rises.
Rush Hour Midwest.
City shunt. Suburban ride.
Blues Brothers movie.

Book at Clark/Division, the Loop.
Book for North side, South side.
Book up to Linden, down to 95th/Dan Ryan.
Book the L. Book Chicago.

Tokyo Crossway

For Shoko Miura

Shibuya no sukuranburu kosaten
Shibuya Crossing.

Metro Tokyo foot passenger hub.
Linear X and Zebra intersection.
Yamanote line Metro.
Hachikō statue dog.
Youth fantasyland.
Fashion plenty.
The Scramble.

A rush-hour day could have you thinking.
Exodus, led by Moses, starring Heston's beard.
Eisenstein filming the Odessa steps in *Potemkin*.
Screen battle lines in *Lord of the Rings*.

A night-time could have you thinking.
Star Wars and its imperial soldiery.
The Matrix and Agent Smith in multiples.
Emptying Shea Stadium rock concert.

High rise Tsutaya Building.
HM Music, UC Credit card.
Calvin Klein jeans commercial.
Eatery, store, neon-lit sublimity.

Watch the same-time change of lights.
Be part of the surge, the milling criss-cross.
Shibuya its own perfect crowd control.
Tokyo its own pedestrian architecture.

Tangier Faith: Le Grand Mosque

For Abdelrrahim Elouahabi and Abdelmajid Elsayd

Literature invented Tangier.

—Khalid Amine

You head for the Souk Dakhel.
You pass Le Central of brasserie fame.
You head for Rue Sheyaghine and Rue Dbagu.
Street, alley, noise, trinket, trade.
The Medina. Le Grand Mosque.

Language overlaps: Darija-Tanjawi, Berber, French.
Histories ply: Phoenicians to the colonial Europeans.
Geographies interact: Les Terraces to the American Legation.
Authorships haunt: Choukri to Bowles and Burroughs.
The Medina. The calls to prayer.

Eyes focus on the Mosque.
No doubt others hold greater sway.
Al-Aqsa or Cairo's Ali Muhammad.
But this is Tangier spiritually at home.
The Medina. Islam within Interzone.

White longitudinal wall.
Dark-green studded doors.
Built extension.
Mohammed VI 2003 plaque to celebrate.
The Medina. Worn edifice. Peelings.

You look upwards to the *sawmaa*.
You contemplate tower, crescent.
You nod to gatekeepers.
Architecture lived, for everyday prayer.
The Medina. Le Grand Mosque.

Sevilla: One and the Same

In memoriam, Gobain Ovejero Zappino

i.
First it's Andalucía, *Ál-Andalus*.
The necessary stereotype.
Flamenco. Plaza de Toros. Gazpacho.

Arts? Of course.
Granada's Lorca, Jaén's Segovia.
Murillo, Velázquez, Picasso.

Then Sevilla. Maybe via Italy and France.
Listen to *Il Barbiere di Siviglia*.
Switch from Rossini to Beaumarchais original.

But Sevilla writes its own city passage.
Roman, Visigoth, Spanish, Moorish, Sephardic, Roma.
Many, singular, a ply of fibre and voice.

ii.
Sevilla: enter time's span of architecture.
La Muralla de la Ciudad, boundary of *época islámica*.
La Exposición de Sevilla, 1992 and new Europe.

Sevilla: enter time's geometries of belief.
Greek Heracles-myth for discovery. Roman Jupiter worship.
Christianity's cross. Islam's Crescent. David's star.

Sevilla: enter time's pageant of glory and shadow.
Trade, port, archive, church, *período cristiano*.
Las Américas. Pogrom. Slave pen. Colony gold.

iii.

The eye takes in *El Real Alcázar.*
How not to be won?
Courtyard gardens four-squared. Orchard. Patio.

Gallery corridors, hedge patterns, guide your walk.
Sour orange and lemon tree give colour and aromatic.
Branches for shade, flowers for beauty.

Almohad and *Mudéjar* architecture.
Reyes Católicos re-conquest and style.
Arab friezes. Spanish tiles. Connecting pools.

You contemplate *El Palacio de Don Pedro,* kingship's luxury.
You roam *El Salón del Almirante,* Spain of sea and discovery.
You even view new Spain, those first, and royal, tennis courts.

But where more to feel art's call than *El Salón de Embajadores?*
Poly-linked arch and column, Kufi Arabic wall script.
Decorative star. Moon crescent. Illuminated faith world.

iv.

Built histories.

La Giralda: Minaret and Bell Tower. Weather vane.
Barrio Santa Cruz: Christian Parish and *Judería*, tourism.
Barrio Triana: Roman, Roma, Craft-worker enclave.
Catedral: Gothic, medieval knave, maybe tomb of Genoa's Columbus.
Plaza de España: Alcoves of Spanish provinces yet footfall of Venice.
Hotel Alfonso XIII: Ceramic splendour. Lebanese cuisine.
Casa de la Memoria, Flamenco's theatre of history.
Las Setas: Metropol Parasol. City-centre. Time-now's market canopy.
Eli Wiesel German camp-survivor river plaque: "Por la tolerancia."
Coup d'Etat French bar. Thompson and Thompson English food store.

"Are you from Peru?" asks the *Norteamericano*
in Seville's Mexican restaurant.
"No" says the waiter, in perfect Cockney English,
"I am from Seville."

Traverse Sevilla, legacies, namings.
Sevilla: Una Misma Cosa.
Seville: many, singular, one and the same.

Chemical Brussels: Atomium

Expo 1958, World's Fair,
and it appeared, shall we say,
with a bang.
Eighteen spheres, escalators, panorama,
then the glitter of steel
to replace the original aluminium.
Iron crystal model from Atomic Number 26
transposed into public sight,
molecule and ion on view.

But the title had you addled.
Wasn't atomic a word itself contaminated?
Atomic Bomb. Atomic Poisoning.
Weren't we in an age talking Strontium 90?
Shadows of Bikini Atoll, Manhattan Project, Hiroshima.
But no, the eye suggested better,
Progressive science. Public Celebration.
Belgian capital pride.
Belgian history display.

So you continue to ponder the implications.
Science from the past.
Science for the future.
Perhaps more you ponder the art.
Architecture and Sculpture.
A dare of construction.
Brussels UFO. *2001* film-corridors.
Molecular, a formula, indeed atomic.
Yet chemistry become imagination's alchemy.

Musée d'Orsay

You know it was the Gare d'Orsay.
Chemin de fer de Paris à Orléans.
An ageing Parisian I met remembered tickets and steam.
But now, he said a touch ruefully, it's a palace of art.
It was better, he added, when it was a station.
Not exactly the standard view.

You meantime do the galleries.
Once platforms hold the barrel interior.
Arch vaulting gives the ceilings.
Triple level collections and displays.
Manet's luncheon to Cézanne's card players.
Whistler's mother to Dégas's absinth.
Van Gogh's skies to Gaugin's Tahiti.
Impressionism's palace. Art Nouveau.
Central Nave sculpture.
Photography and Drawings.
Architecture itself in design, map, model.
Station to museum, 1986 and Opening.
Left Bank Paris triumph.

You take respite, eye sated.
Or almost.
There's yet the building.
Stately, ornate, elongated.
Daytime or night-lit a windowed cloister.

You think to connect tickets of train and exhibit.
History's different stations.
Then you eye the clocks.
Or more to the point the clock faces.

Interiors and exteriors.
Beauteous whether gilded or line-sharp.
Guardian time-keepers.
Travel and museum.
Imagination and gallery.
Two kinds of rail art.

Welsh Windows

Aunt by marriage, a shared surname.
But an artist, a painter, was anomaly in my family.
1920s design school, then that North Wales studio.
Converted chapel, organ loft for brush and easel.
Place-name a joy of Welsh spelling.
Garndolbenmaen.
With Snowdonia's *Moel Hebog* a hill horizon.
She painted walls, flowers, valleys, sun streaks.
There were rivulets, an occasion leap of fish or bird.
Plus the human figures, decked-out or nude.

One canvas lingers.
A house transposed from down the lane to canvas.
The original under the name of much aged Miss Williams.
Hers a family Williams among the nearby over-dozen.
The dwelling, cottage-style, was tight packed granite.
Local quarried. Barely cemented.
Russet, mossy, with sloping roof of grey-blue slate.

The portrait was dutiful if hardly Golden Age Flemish.
Miss Williams, crooked, in wellingtons, came to inspect.
Accented, a native speaker, she glared and tutted.
Her verdict was summary, judicial.
"My house," she said, full of custody,
"has *five* windows not *four*."
Right she was. *Five. Pedwar* in her mother tongue.

It was a moment to store in memory.
To keep for time and countries, time and galleries.
Each later viewing of art and architecture.

The Actual and the Image.
Not a pipe said Magritte.
Art and Illusion said Gombrich.
Ways of Seeing and About Looking said Berger.

Aunt and Miss Williams had been there.

Whose windows?

Architectures Unseen

Nightmare Sakhalin
One day I'll go there.
A visit-dip into gulag nightmare.
Island penal colony.
Tsarist paw mark.
Stalin's Soviet hell.
You read it in Chekhov.
You read it in Solzhenitsyn.
There's *ainu* in the story.
There are Japan and Korea in the story.
And modern oil-energy and downed Air Flight 007.
But the fences and huts remain, accuse.
Far Russia.
Sakhalin: history's prison shadow.

Yemeni Highrise
One day I'll go there.
Shibam tower city.
Manhattan of the Desert they say.
Mud-brick ancient height.
Yet skyscraper-balcony modern.
Brown storey, white topped.
Ancestral with air-conditioning.
Walled enclave of life and poem.
Before Islam.
After Al Qaeda.
Arabian grid, contiguity, clay.
Built for defence, trade.
Built, vertically, of peninsular time.

Dream Brasilia
One day I'll go there.
Niemeyer 1950s modernism.

Utopia-urban Brazil.
Yet elegant monotony said de Beauvoir.
Superquadras—spatial, airy.
Eixo Monumental—avenue and width.
Cathedral—upward curved, asparagus.
Congress—upright H with side dishes.
Central Bank—block design.
Kubitschek Bridge—wave-pattern and girder.
Airport—leaning window and light-perfect.
So *Brasilia,* how best to know?
Built full or empty?

About the Poet

A. ROBERT LEE was a professor in the English department at Nihon University from 1997-2011. British-born, he previously taught at the University of Kent, UK. His creative work includes *Japan Textures: Sight and Word,* with Mark Gresham (2007), *Tokyo Commute: Japanese Customs and Way of Life Viewed from the Odakyu Line* (2011), and the verse collections *Ars Geographica: Maps and Compasses* (2012), *Portrait and Landscape: Further Geographies* (2013), *Imaginarium: Sightings, Galleries, Sightlines* (2013), *Americas: Selected Verse and Vignette* (2015), *Password: A Book of Locks and Keys* (2016) and *Off Course: Roundabouts & Deviations* (2016). Among his academic publications are *Multicultural American Literature: Comparative Black, Native, Latino/a and Asian Fictions* (2003), which won the American Book Award in 2004, and *Modern American Counter Writing: Beats, Outriders, Ethnics* (2010). Currently he lives in Murcia, Spain. ❐

Other Books By 2Leaf Press

2LEAF PRESS challenges the status quo by publishing alternative fiction, non-fiction, poetry and bilingual works by activists, academics, poets and authors dedicated to diversity and social justice with scholarship that is accessible to the general public. 2LEAF PRESS produces high quality and beautifully produced hardcover, paperback and ebook formats through our series: *2LP Explorations in Diversity*, *2LP University Books*, *2LP Classics*, *2LP Translations*, *Nuyorican World Series*, and *2LP Current Affairs, Culture & Politics*. Below is a selection of 2LEAF PRESS' published titles.

2LP EXPLORATIONS IN DIVERSITY

Substance of Fire: Gender and Race in the College Classroom
by Claire Millikin
Foreword by R. Joseph Rodríguez, Afterword by Richard Delgado
Contributed material by Riley Blanks, Blake Calhoun, Rox Trujillo

Black Lives Have Always Mattered
A Collection of Essays, Poems, and Personal Narratives
Edited by Abiodun Oyewole

The Beiging of America:
Personal Narratives about Being Mixed Race in the 21st Century
Edited by Cathy J. Schlund-Vials, Sean Frederick Forbes, Tara Betts
with an Afterword by Heidi Durrow

What Does it Mean to be White in America?
Breaking the White Code of Silence, A Collection of Personal Narratives
Edited by Gabrielle David and Sean Frederick Forbes
Introduction by Debby Irving and Afterword by Tara Betts

2LP UNIVERSITY BOOKS
Designs of Blackness, Mappings in the Literature and
Culture of African Americans
A. Robert Lee
20TH ANNIVERSARY EXPANDED EDITION

2LP CLASSICS
Adventures in Black and White
Edited and with a critical introduction by Tara Betts
by Philippa Duke Schuyler

Monsters: Mary Shelley's Frankenstein and Mathilda
by Mary Shelley, edited by Claire Millikin Raymond

2LP TRANSLATIONS
Birds on the Kiswar Tree
by Odi Gonzales, Translated by Lynn Levin
Bilingual: English/Spanish

Incessant Beauty, A Bilingual Anthology
by Ana Rossetti, Edited and Translated by Carmela Ferradáns
Bilingual: English/Spanish

NUYORICAN WORLD SERIES
Our Nuyorican Thing, The Birth of a Self-Made Identity
by Samuel Carrion Diaz, with an Introduction by Urayoán Noel
Bilingual: English/Spanish

Hey Yo! Yo Soy!, 40 Years of Nuyorican Street Poetry,
The Collected Works of Jesús Papoleto Meléndez
Bilingual: English/Spanish

LITERARY NONFICTION
No Vacancy; Homeless Women in Paradise
by Michael Reid

The Beauty of Being, A Collection of Fables, Short Stories & Essays
by Abiodun Oyewole

WHEREABOUTS: Stepping Out of Place,
An Outside in Literary & Travel Magazine Anthology
Edited by Brandi Dawn Henderson

PLAYS
Rivers of Women, The Play
by Shirley Bradley LeFlore, with photographs by Michael J. Bracey

AUTOBIOGRAPHIES/MEMOIRS/BIOGRAPHIES
Trailblazers, Black Women Who Helped Make America Great
American Firsts/American Icons
by Gabrielle David

Mother of Orphans
The True and Curious Story of Irish Alice, A Colored Man's Widow
by Dedria Humphries Barker

Strength of Soul
by Naomi Raquel Enright

Dream of the Water Children:
Memory and Mourning in the Black Pacific
by Fredrick D. Kakinami Cloyd
Foreword by Velina Hasu Houston, Introduction by Gerald Horne
Edited by Karen Chau

The Fourth Moment: Journeys from the Known to the Unknown, A Memoir
by Carole J. Garrison, Introduction by Sarah Willis

POETRY
PAPOLíTICO, Poems of a Political Persuasion
by Jesús Papoleto Meléndez
with an Introduction by Joel Kovel and DeeDee Halleck

Critics of Mystery Marvel, Collected Poems
by Youssef Alaoui, with an Introduction by Laila Halaby

shrimp
by jason vasser-elong, with an Introduction by Michael Castro
The Revlon Slough, New and Selected Poems
by Ray DiZazzo, with an Introduction by Claire Millikin

Written Eye: Visuals/Verse
by A. Robert Lee

A Country Without Borders: Poems and Stories of Kashmir
by Lalita Pandit Hogan, with an Introduction by Frederick Luis Aldama

Branches of the Tree of Life
The Collected Poems of Abiodun Oyewole 1969-2013
by Abiodun Oyewole, edited by Gabrielle David
with an Introduction by Betty J. Dopson

2Leaf Press is an imprint owned and operated by the Intercultural Alliance of Artists & Scholars, Inc. (IAAS), a NY-based nonprofit organization that publishes and promotes multicultural literature.

NEW YORK
www.2leafpress.org